Inspirations From Scotland
Vol II
Edited by Mark Richardson

First published in Great Britain in 2007 by:
Young Writers
Remus House
Coltsfoot Drive
Peterborough
PE2 9JX
Telephone: 01733 890066
Website: www.youngwriters.co.uk

All Rights Reserved

© *Copyright Contributors 2007*

SB ISBN 978-1 84431 227 6

For

Young Writers was es
been passionately dev
reading and writing in
ever since. The ques
Writers remains as cor
poetic and literary talent as ever.

This year's Young Writers competition has proven as vibrant and dynamic as ever and we are delighted to present a showcase of the best poetry from across the UK and in some cases overseas. Each poem has been selected from a wealth of *Little Laureates* entries before ultimately being published in this, our sixteenth primary school poetry series.

Once again, we have been supremely impressed by the overall quality of the entries we have received. The imagination, energy and creativity which has gone into each young writer's entry made choosing the poems a challenging and often difficult but ultimately hugely rewarding task - the general high standard of the work submitted ensured this opportunity to bring their poetry to a larger appreciative audience.

We sincerely hope you are pleased with this final collection and that you will enjoy *Little Laureates Inspirations From Scotland Vol II* for many years to come.

Contents

Balfron Primary School, Glasgow
Emily Wilson (9)	1
Rhiannon McAra (10)	2
Ethan Smith (10)	3
Emma Boyle (9)	4
Ben McGuire (9)	5
Maisie Price (9)	6
Christine Steel (9)	7
Euan Gray (9)	8
Taylor Rice (9)	9
Tom Chandler (9)	10
Anna Thomson (9)	11
Molly Smith (9)	12
Ross MacKenzie (9)	13
Lewis McGuire (9)	14
Rebecca Gage (9)	15
Finlay Mann (8)	16
Chiara Tortolano (10)	17
Gillian Gray (9)	18
Jamie Arnold (9)	19
Johnathan McGuire (9)	20
Kalim McDonagh (9)	21
Rachel Morris (9)	22
Jack McGibbon (9)	23

Blacklaw Primary School, Glasgow
Craig McKerlie (11)	24
Fiona Irving (11)	25
Andrew McMorris (11)	26
Jacob Jacobs (11)	27
Jordan Barrie (12)	28

Blackwood Primary School, Lanark
Andrew Dunlop (9)	29
Jordan Crilly (9)	30
David Murray (9)	31
Sophie Campbell (10)	32
Ben Smith (9)	33

Marie McBride (10)	34
Emma Brown (9)	35
Calum Smith (10)	36
Justin Simpson (9)	37
Kerin Sneddon (10)	38
Hannah Crooks (9)	39
Jack Rollo (9)	40
Katie McGettigan (9)	41
Lowri Shearer (10)	42
Megan Carty (9)	43
Jennifer Alexander (9)	44
Colin Wilson (9)	45
David Leavy (9)	46
Jack Lyttle (9)	47
Nicole Gardiner (10)	48
Jay Wilson (10)	49
Katie Garrity (9)	50
Katie Hindley (10)	51
Paige Murphy (11)	52
Jason Simpson (10)	53
Sean Corrigan (9)	54
Caitlin Woodside (10)	55
Lisa Lockhart (11)	56
Meg Ross (10)	57
Rebecca Millward (10)	58
Jordan Millward (10)	59
Alex Jenkinson (10)	60

Cathedral Primary School, Motherwell

Beth Cunningham (8)	61
Konner Millar-Brookbanks (9)	62
Carla Tyrrell (9)	63
Owen Leach (8)	64
Georgia Deerin (8)	65

East Plean Primary School, Stirling

Courteney Williamson (9)	66
Darren Gerrard (9)	67
Llyam Valentine (9)	68
Ryan Curran (9)	69
Ivor Swan (9)	70

Zaynab Akhtar (9)	71
Chelsea Hart Donald (9)	72
Megan Elvin (9)	73

Greenhills Primary School, East Kilbride

Amy-Leigh McDade (10)	74
Samantha McLean (10)	75
Shannon Gair (11)	76
Lauren McWhinnie (10)	77
Kalina Ritchie (11)	78
Ewan Gardiner (10)	79
Amy Platt (11)	80
Sarah Sanders (10)	81
Josh Cecchetti (10)	82
Alicia McNab (11)	83

Lenzie Primary School, Glasgow

Stuart Frame (8)	84
Olivia Gibson (9)	85
Matthew Wan (8)	86
Ayan Shaukat (9)	87
Inayah Jamil (9)	88
Saoirse Murdoch (8)	89
Gavin Williams (9)	90
Alex Tomkins (9)	91
Findlay Clark (8)	92
Ben McLean (8)	93

Lumphinnans Primary School, Lumphinnans

Kim Ritchie (11)	94
Amy Moir (11)	95
Laura Brown (11)	96
Caitlin Burns (11)	97
Shannon Watson (11)	98
Nicole Brogan (11)	99
Nicole Moffat (11)	100
Sarah Venters (12)	101
Kelly Maxwell (11)	102
Nathan Kernaghan (11)	103
Michael Sutherland (9)	104
Dylan Evans (10)	105

Brandon Henderson (10)	106
Rebecca McAllister (9)	107
Chelsea Muir (9)	108
Mhari Wilson (9)	109
Ailidh Ferguson (9)	110
Amy Simpson (9)	111
Amy Howie (9)	112
Ryan Menzies (10)	113
Rhys Connor (9)	114
Christopher Davies (10)	115
James Merrilees (9)	116
Blair Jones (10)	117
Alisha McAllister (9)	118
Natalie Wilson (12)	119

Morningside Primary School, Wishaw

Erika Black (9)	120
Mark Bradshaw (8)	121
Grant Wood (9)	122
Katherine Colvin (9)	123
Robert Crawford (9)	124
Alastair Macfarlane (9)	125
Lauren Daly & Lucy Burns (11)	126

Murray Primary School, East Kilbride

Sophie Macinnes (9)	127
Euan Hamilton (9)	128
Ross MacGregor (10)	129
James Nugent (10)	130
Laura Gillies (10)	131
Lara Wark (10)	132
Nikki Forsyth (10)	133
Bethan Mackie (11)	134
Alison Lovatt (10)	135
Rebecca McNally (11)	136
Emma Devine (9)	137
Jennifer Mackie (9)	138
Owen Garrity (9)	139
Kirstin Hosie (9)	140
Melissa Green (10)	141
John Murphy (9)	142

Robyn Graham (9) 143
Courtney Smith (9) 144
Emily McNeill (9) 145
Josh Renicks (9) 146
Ewan Gamble (9) 147
Conor Campbell (10) 148
Rebecca Bogle (9) 149
Ellis Donald (9) 150

St Gregory's Primary School, Glasgow
Kloi Graikos (10) 151
Sean Hope (10) 152
Nicole Hampson (10) 153
Caitlin Mitchell (10) 154
Stephanie Galloway (10) 155
Shannyn Strickland (10) 156

Strathburn School, Inverurie
Fraser Yule (10) 157
Callum Jones (9) 158
Alana Williams (9) 159
Hayley McKay (9) 160
Hannah Garden (10) 161
Jacqueline McKeown (9) 162
Greg Center (10) 163
Nadia Inglis (10) 164

West Kilbride Primary School, West Kilbride
Rebecca Brown (11) 165
Rachael Miller (11) 166
Gordon Wilson (11) 167
Clark Ferguson (11) 168
Melissa Coby (11) 169
Kerr Wilson (11) 170
Kate Parker (8) 171
Sam Edwards (7) 172
Fraser Murray (7) 173
Caitlin McMail (7) 174
Thomas Orr (8) 175
Erin English (8) 176
Abbie Fairclough (8) 177

Jacob McBain (8)	178
Josef Bacon (7)	179
Emily McAlpine (8)	180
Ross Maclean (7)	181
Cerys Seaton (8)	182
Emma Turner (7)	183
Heather McClymont (11)	184
Sarah Wanless (11)	185
Sarah Davies (11)	186
Jonathan Revie (11)	187
Amy Hands (10)	188
Catherine Bacon (10)	189
Ross Wilson (10)	190
Tom Hunt (10)	191
Rachel Stirling (11)	192
Jennifer Green (11)	193
Gemma MacMaster (11)	194
Emily Brittan (11)	195
Euan Mitchell (11)	196
Katie Powell (11)	197
Sean Rees (11)	198
Iona Lennie (11)	199

The Poems

Hate

Hate sounds like people
Shouting in my little ear.
Hate tastes like tears rushing
From my eyes.

Hate smells like coldness
Flowing through the air.
Hate tastes like people
Fighting round and round
The street.

Hate feels like tenseness
Filing up my small face
Hate reminds me of a really hated moment
That has haunted me since the day it happened.

Emily Wilson (9)
Balfron Primary School, Glasgow

Happiness

Happiness sounds like golden bells ringing and pretty birds singing,
Happiness tastes like yummy yellow bananas and steaming hot food
off a bbq.
Happiness smells like the salty seaside air and lavender blossoming
In a field of flowers,
Happiness looks like soft warm sand and fluffy white clouds,
Happiness feels lovely and joyful, and it warms your heart,
Happiness reminds me of swimming in the warm sea and distant
memories with my dad.
Happiness is great!

Rhiannon McAra (10)
Balfron Primary School, Glasgow

Love

Love sounds like sitting next to a warm fire and
Listening to romantic music.

Love tastes like eating strawberry hearts and
Walking on green summery grass.

Love smells like a million pounds.

Love looks like a warm heart getting bigger and bigger.

Love feels like a cute baby puppy
That has just been born.

Love reminds me of a hot sunny beach
Next to a gentle ocean.

Ethan Smith (10)
Balfron Primary School, Glasgow

Happiness

Happiness sounds like
Leaves crinkling as they fall to the ground.

Happiness tastes like
Melted chocolate dipped in marshmallows.

Happiness smells like
The gentle cold air.

Happiness looks like
People eating ice cream and having fun.

Happiness feels like
Floating in the calm sea.

Happiness reminds me of
Long sunny holidays on the beach.

Emma Boyle (9)
Balfron Primary School, Glasgow

Happiness

Happiness sounds like people laughing and splashing about
In warm water.

Happiness tastes like chocolate melting in
My mouth.

Happiness smells like the salty breeze
Next to the seashore.

Happiness looks like people playing and having fun.

Happiness feels like being joyful
And being happy.

Happiness reminds me of vanilla ice cream.

Ben McGuire (9)
Balfron Primary School, Glasgow

Love

Love sounds like a newborn lamb freshly born in spring,
Love tastes like a juicy strawberry from a lovely cold, fresh box,
Love smells like pretty blossom of a summer flower,
Love looks like a red, red rose,
Love feels like a soft, silky pillow that's rubbing on my cheek,
Love reminds me of the happy times I had with my mum.

Maisie Price (9)
Balfron Primary School, Glasgow

Sadness

Sadness tastes
So hard and bland
Like all important
Things have gone.

Sadness feels like
Pins and needles
Digging in so hard
So painfully.

Sadness looks like
People upset or ill
Who simply need
A helping hand.

Sadness sounds like
Crying and shouting
So loud and frustrated.

Sadness smells like
Hot out-of-date milk
So mouldy and ever so green.

Sadness reminds me
Of poor people younger
Or older dying of
Thirst and hunger.

Christine Steel (9)
Balfron Primary School, Glasgow

Fear

Fear sounds like Darth Vader breathing,
Fear tastes of hot chilli peppers diving down my throat,
Fear smells of somebody throwing up,
Fear looks like a skull and crossbones,
Fear feels like lava burning my hands,
Fear reminds me of getting run over by a car.

Euan Gray (9)
Balfron Primary School, Glasgow

Happiness

Happiness sounds like me and my friends giggling at a sleepover.
Happiness tastes like creamy chocolate smothered
                                             with marshmallows.
Happiness smells like sweet flowers swaying in the park.
Happiness looks like a big group of puppies barking at me.
Happiness feels like soft, fluffy teddies rubbing on my face.
Happiness reminds me of colourful rainbows in the bright blue sky.

Taylor Rice (9)
Balfron Primary School, Glasgow

Sadness

Sadness feels like you are covered in spikes,
Sadness tastes like cold, mushy peas,
Sadness sounds like a little girl,
Screaming in a small dark corner,
Sadness smells like a rotten bird,
Sadness looks like a broken ornament,
Sadness reminds me of the death of my grandmother.

Tom Chandler (9)
Balfron Primary School, Glasgow

Sorrow

Sorrow sounds like heavy raindrops banging onto the ground,
Sorrow tastes like cold dry chalk in my warm wet mouth,
Sorrow smells like a landfill site filled with people's memories,
Sorrow feels like a cold sharp dagger sticking into my straight,
                                                                            cold back,
Sorrow reminds me of *death*.
I hate sorrow.

Anna Thomson (9)
Balfron Primary School, Glasgow

Sadness

Sadness sounds like crying with tears streaming down my cheek
Slowly and carefully.

Sadness feels uncomfortable like things sharp and rough
Digging into me like hailstones hitting my nose, sore and painfully.

Sadness looks like people upset and ill
Like poor people who don't have things that we have.

Sadness tastes like the last chunk of Easter egg melting in my
Mouth, so yummy and chocolatey.

Sadness reminds me of people ill and death:
Like things important to me have gone.

I hate sadness!

Molly Smith (9)
Balfron Primary School, Glasgow

Sadness

Sadness sounds like crying at a family's funeral.
Sadness tastes like tears running from their eyes.
Sadness smells like smoke and fire.
Sadness looks like people dying horribly.
Sadness feels like rainclouds over my head.
Sadness reminds me of loss of family.

Ross MacKenzie (9)
Balfron Primary School, Glasgow

Anger

Anger sounds like many people screaming and shouting,
Anger tastes like burning fireballs in your mouth,
Anger smells like red fire gas spreading everywhere,
Anger looks like a giant volcano erupting,
Anger feels like many needles jagging into you,
Anger reminds me of hating and loving at the same time.

Lewis McGuire (9)
Balfron Primary School, Glasgow

Happiness

Happiness sounds like warm water splashing and smooth yellow sand swishing on the shore,

Happiness tastes like chicken noodles from SeeWoo and Warm chocolate fudge cake for dessert,

Happiness smells like my mum's vanilla perfume She puts on before she goes out,

Happiness looks like our kind, grateful, family playing happily Together on the warm, sandy beach,

Happiness feels like my warm teddy bears and my green fluffy
                                                                                pillows,
Happiness reminds me of our great fun and fantastic holiday
                                                                               to Menorca.

I love happiness, it will never fade away . . .

Rebecca Gage (9)
Balfron Primary School, Glasgow

Sadness

Sadness sounds like lots of people crying and screaming in the
                                                    night-time darkness,
Sadness tastes like the tears from your eyes as salty as the sea,
Sadness smells like a horrible dump stinking of old rubbish
                                                    with old food,
Sadness looks like people sad and crying with unhappy faces,
Sadness feels like you're always left out of things all the time,
Sadness reminds me of sad programmes and lots of people dying.

Finlay Mann (8)
Balfron Primary School, Glasgow

Love

Love sounds like happy people singing and dancing,
Love tastes like chocolate and pasta with butter,
Love smells like Diesel perfume,
Love looks like a ring of some sort,
Love feels like soft, smooth silk,
Love reminds me of a love heart.

Chiara Tortolano (10)
Balfron Primary School, Glasgow

Love

Love sounds like people talking and sharing their loving words.
Love tastes like nothing ever tasted before.
Love smells like human's perfume and deodorant scents lying on the sofa.
Love looks like lipstick lying on a man's face.
Love feels like a very soft and smooth silk bedcover.
Love reminds me of men and women holding their beautiful newborn babies.

Gillian Gray (9)
Balfron Primary School, Glasgow

Love Poem

Love feels like big love hearts floating in the sky,
Love smells like blossom falling off a tree,
Love looks like fluffy clouds floating in the blue sky,
Love reminds me of cooking, mouth-watering marshmallows,
Love tastes like pink fizzy sweets.

Jamie Arnold (9)
Balfron Primary School, Glasgow

Hate

Hate sounds like people screaming and shouting at each other
In the street on a wet, rainy night.
Hate tastes like wet gritty wood grinding in my teeth.
Hate smells like smoky coal seeping through the air.
Hate looks like a cold wet person standing behind rusted metal bars.
Hate feels like you are being controlled and it gives you the
Temptation to rip them apart.
Hate reminds me of someone gasping in anger.

Johnathan McGuire (9)
Balfron Primary School, Glasgow

Anger

Anger sounds like a devil's scream
While waiting for another person to come
To their lair.

Anger tastes like a sour old mint.

Anger smells like an old disgusting
Landfill site.

Anger looks like a burning chamber deep underground.

Anger feels like a hot, hot brand against my cheek.

Anger reminds me of a big petrifying fight.

Kalim McDonagh (9)
Balfron Primary School, Glasgow

Anger

Anger sounds like a devil's high-pitched screaming,
Anger feels like a fire, roaring and beaming,
Anger smells like an old rotten boot,
Anger tastes like a frog's slimy old foot,
Anger looks like a big, dark room,
Anger reminds me of people locked up in a tomb.

Rachel Morris (9)
Balfron Primary School, Glasgow

Talent

Talent sounds like music to my ears
Talent tastes like lovely strawberries
Talent smells like florist bouquets
Talent looks like a magnificent stallion
Talent feels like soft feathers
Talent reminds me of love.

Jack McGibbon (9)
Balfron Primary School, Glasgow

The Anteater - Haiku

Claws to rip off bark
It feasts on thousands of ants
Sticky long red tongue.

Craig McKerlie (11)
Blacklaw Primary School, Glasgow

White Water Bird - Haiku

Cygnets swimming near
Feathers as white as snowflakes
Long straight, white, smooth neck.

Fiona Irving (11)
Blacklaw Primary School, Glasgow

Lion - Haiku

King of the jungle,
Hunts prey with sharp claws and teeth,
A fierce animal.

Andrew McMorris (11)
Blacklaw Primary School, Glasgow

My Dog Maggie - Haiku

Frantically jumping
Like a taunted bull raging
Blonde bundle of fun.

Jacob Jacobs (11)
Blacklaw Primary School, Glasgow

Ella - Haiku

Big eyes and brown fur
Small fluffy ears like pillows
White teeth like needles.

Jordan Barrie (12)
Blacklaw Primary School, Glasgow

Untitled

I feel excited when I enter the dark wardrobe
I feel weird when I enter the dark wardrobe
I feel anxious when I enter the wardrobe
I feel scared when I enter the wardrobe
I feel happy when I enter the wardrobe
I feel worried when I enter the wardrobe.

Andrew Dunlop (9)
Blackwood Primary School, Lanark

My Spring Poem

When winter comes
I always think of spring.
I see flowers blooming in the distance.
I see frogspawn bright as I walk past a pond.
I smell the fresh air which is quite refreshing
In all ways.
I can smell a barbecue burning as my next door neighbour
Is cooking dinner for the family.
As I run through a field to see my family,
A bee stings me and I shout as loud as I can.
I can see my family coming towards me.

Jordan Crilly (9)
Blackwood Primary School, Lanark

How I Feel

I felt curious when I went into the dark classroom
I felt surprised when I saw the half-man, half-animal
I felt nervous when the class went under the bin bags
I felt delighted at the wardrobe that was deep and dark
I felt joyful going into the cave
I felt jumpy when I went into the classroom
I felt excited at the teacher reading the book
I felt happy because it was awfully dark.

David Murray (9)
Blackwood Primary School, Lanark

My Feelings Poem!

I felt anxious when I walked into the wardrobe.
I felt excited walking through the smooth coats.
I felt puzzled when it was all dark and scary.
I felt hot sitting in the big, dark tunnel.
I felt cold sitting in the cold, creepy forest.
I felt sad when the foal started crying.
I felt shocked to do something I don't usually do.
I felt curious walking through the big green bushes.

Sophie Campbell (10)
Blackwood Primary School, Lanark

The View From My Window

My windows are wide.
I can see fields, big and short.
Sometimes I stare, I can just make out a scarecrow
Waving to me as I go by.
I can see big and short houses with brick patterns.
All different shapes and sizes.
As cars come out of their drives and I wave to them
As I go by.

Ben Smith (9)
Blackwood Primary School, Lanark

Springtime

Springtime is here.
The flowers are growing.
Lambs and baby animals are born.
It is fantastic.

I hear the sounds of chicks tweeting
And branches on trees swaying in the breeze.
The baby pigs snorting
And the blast of the music playing in the background.

I smell the cut grass.
I am swimming in the fresh air.
I smell the barbecue that people are having.

I feel joyful the summer holidays are finally here.
I feel lonely that everyone is away on holiday.

Marie McBride (10)
Blackwood Primary School, Lanark

My Spring Poem

In spring a flower grows and a cool breeze blows.
The birds singing beautifully as the sun shining lovingly
And the farmer goes out and feeds his animals.
The children playing loudly and happily.
And all I will choose is spring, spring, spring.
The thing that I smell most is fresh air everywhere I go.

Emma Brown (9)
Blackwood Primary School, Lanark

I Feel Sad

I feel sad when someone else gets the glory.
I smell bad goings on in the atmosphere.
I see another person getting their hand raised.
I hear a whole new interest starting.
I touch the ground when I am lying down.

Calum Smith (10)
Blackwood Primary School, Lanark

Spring Poem

The sun is out the sky is blue
There's not a cloud to spoil the view
I'm tired when I come in from playing out
I eat some sweets then drink, then I go out to play
I feel happy playing with my friends and going out and about.

Justin Simpson (9)
Blackwood Primary School, Lanark

My Poem

I feel excited when I went through the coat stand.
I feel happy when we went in the wardrobe.
I feel anxious when we were reading in the corridor.
I feel very pleased when we went outside.
I feel joyful when we were sitting in the wardrobe.
I feel surprised when we went through the scary coat stand.
I feel delighted because I had done it.
I feel sad because some people got sent out.

Kerin Sneddon (10)
Blackwood Primary School, Lanark

Feelings

I feel happy touching fur and fleece
I feel nervous when the wardrobe goes on and on
I feel surprised crawling under dark bin bags.

I feel excited feeling mud and stones underneath me
I feel cold feeling leaves and branches
I feel happy listening to the teacher reading a story.

I feel comforted by the music
I feel good writing this poem.

Hannah Crooks (9)
Blackwood Primary School, Lanark

Feelings In My Journey

I felt excited when we entered the deep dark cave.

I felt nervous when we went through the cloakroom
Of different sizes of coats.

It felt different when we sat down in the cold forest.

I felt joyful when I entered the huge wardrobes.

I felt frightened when the faun didn't even know
I was human or an animal.

I felt annoyed when I slipped and nearly fell in the forest.

I felt scared as soon as I heard about what the faun looked like.

I felt famous when I met the faun because no other human
Would have seen one.

Jack Rollo (9)
Blackwood Primary School, Lanark

Sad

Sadness is when I have no one to play with
I see tears about to fall from my eyes
I hear people talking about me
I smell smoke in my room, I wonder if it's my mind
I touch my teddy and sit and cry
I taste mud in my mouth because I was tripped up at school
It's not fair on me.

Katie McGettigan (9)
Blackwood Primary School, Lanark

Scared

Scared is when you're alone in the dark.
I see nothing.
I taste horrible fingernails.
I hear footsteps coming up the hall.
I smell the fresh air from the window.
I touch cold skin.

Lowri Shearer (10)
Blackwood Primary School, Lanark

Happy

Happy is when I am with my friends
I see people playing happily in the sun
I hear people giggling and having fun
I smell children baking cakes
I touch my smiling face
I taste chocolate cake.

Megan Carty (9)
Blackwood Primary School, Lanark

Calm

Calm is when I am fast asleep.
I smell my mum's candles.
I taste fresh water.
I see beautiful colours.
I touch my teddy's soft fur.
I hear the wind outside.

Jennifer Alexander (9)
Blackwood Primary School, Lanark

Anger

Anger is blood warming.
I taste blood from my bleeding nose.
I hear blood dripping in the puddle below me.
I see fire in my eyes.
I touch my bloody nose.

Colin Wilson (9)
Blackwood Primary School, Lanark

Bored

Bored is when the school bell rings
I see my work on my table
I taste yucky tuna
I hear the end of lunch
I touch my language work
I smell a fire in the school - yippee!

David Leavy (9)
Blackwood Primary School, Lanark

Anger

Anger is boiling red fire ready to burst in your own face.
I hate the taste of blood, yuck it's in my mouth.
I see fiery-red because I don't have my own football.
I smell red blood in the air.
I touch red blood when it comes out of my mouth.

Jack Lyttle (9)
Blackwood Primary School, Lanark

Bored

Bored is when you have nothing to do.
I taste the sweets I had at playtime.
I touch boring old maths.
I smell old paint drying up in the corridor.
I hear the teacher shouting at the children.
I see the teacher writing on the blackboard.

Nicole Gardiner (10)
Blackwood Primary School, Lanark

Sad

I feel sad when someone else gets the glory.
I smell bad goings on in the atmosphere.
I see another person getting their hand raised.
I hear a whole new interest starting.
I touch the ground when I am lying down.

Jay Wilson (10)
Blackwood Primary School, Lanark

My Garden

Above my garden
    Are birds singing
        In the sky.

Surrounding my garden
    Is jagged fencing
        In the ground.

Beside my garden
    Are chickens clucking
        In the hut.

Near my garden
    Are machines buzzing
        In the building site.

Katie Garrity (9)
Blackwood Primary School, Lanark

Proud

Proud is head lifting,
I taste bacon sandwiches (when I'm finished)
I hear clapping doing a clap of honour
I touch Flora's big black coat
I smell cups of coffee.

Katie Hindley (10)
Blackwood Primary School, Lanark

Anger

Anger is boiling red steam
I taste smoke of a fire
I see dark blood-red
I touch my warm face
I hear fire crackling
I smell the blood from my bleeding lip.

Paige Murphy (11)
Blackwood Primary School, Lanark

Anger

Anger is when I don't get a sticker
I see blood over people
I taste blood from my tooth
I hear shouting
I touch my fist to stop it hitting
I smell a fiery furnace.

Jason Simpson (10)
Blackwood Primary School, Lanark

My Football Pitch

Above my football pitch
Are floodlights glowing
In the sky.

Beside my football pitch
Are cars parking
In the car park.

Around my football pitch
Are fans cheering
In the stands.

On my football pitch
Are footballers playing
In the grounds.

Below my football pitch
Are moles hunting
In the ground.

Sean Corrigan (9)
Blackwood Primary School, Lanark

Scared

Scared is when I am alone in the dark.
I see something that is shaped like a witch.
I hear the tree banging on my window.
I taste my fingernails when I am biting them.
I smell the sweet smell of my pillow when
My head is under it.
I touch the switch on my lamp as I am about
To turn it on because I am that scared.

Caitlin Woodside (10)
Blackwood Primary School, Lanark

My School

Above my school
   Are birds flying
      In the blue sky.

Beside my school
   Are children running
      In the playground.

Below my school
   Are stones crunching
      In the mud.

Inside my school
   Are tables moving
      In the bases.

Lisa Lockhart (11)
Blackwood Primary School, Lanark

Angry

Anger is for boiling hot red
I see red
I taste blood from my bitten lip
I hear people talking about me
I smell smoke from the fire
I touch a fiery steamy plate.

Meg Ross (10)
Blackwood Primary School, Lanark

Happy

Happy is when you win a football match.
I hear fans cheering in the stands.
I see players running to me when I score a goal.
I touch my medal when I get one.
I taste my water in my bottle.
I smell the burgers that the fans are eating.

Rebecca Millward (10)
Blackwood Primary School, Lanark

Bored

Bored is doing nothing.
I see black and white everywhere.
I taste paper when someone reads a book to me.
I hear people say 'aw' because they are bored.
I touch wooden tables next to me.
I smell rotten apples in the fruit bin.

Jordan Millward (10)
Blackwood Primary School, Lanark

The Dark Place

I feel scared because it was dark and it felt tight.
I feel curious because I'd never been there before.
I feel shocked we don't usually do that.
I feel happy because we missed religious education.
I feel sad because we can't go in the bushes.
I feel excited because it was sweaty.
I feel nervous because we didn't know what would happen.
I feel fun because we had to listen to a book.

Alex Jenkinson (10)
Blackwood Primary School, Lanark

When I Am Tall

When I am tall and the trees are small, there are lots of things that I want to do,
And now is the time to tell you.
These things will make my dreams come true.

I want to be a gymnastic coach and do forward flips to musical notes.
Teaching people to do handstands, that will make me feel very grand.
I want to own a gymnastic club and teach people to do very high jumps.
When people can do stunts like me I'm sure they will be jumping with glee.
After that I will become famous and rich for only doing some twirly flips!
I will feel very happy and excited inside, I will be so tired from stretching so hard,
But it will be good for a healthy heart.
I will buy a castle that is very tall, and will live in it feeling so small.
I will have a butler who will bring me my tea,
That I will drink beside a cherry tree.

I can't wait to grow up and be very tall.
Too bad I am still very small!

Beth Cunningham (8)
Cathedral Primary School, Motherwell

When I Am Tall

When I am tall,
Life will be a ball.
There's lots of things I can do,
Some might even surprise you.

I could work for MI6,
And try out all my sneaky tricks.
I would crawl through air-vents fast,
Avoiding lasers as they blast.

I could be an actor,
And be rich,
But what if my career plunged into a ditch.

I could be an author,
And write a book about bowling.
I'd love to be
Like J K Rowling.

I would live in a mansion,
In Los Angeles,
And in the garden
I would grow palm trees.

I might be a singer,
I just hope my friends will linger.

Now when I am older
I'll be a little bit responsible,
And a little bolder.

Konner Millar-Brookbanks (9)
Cathedral Primary School, Motherwell

My Special Day

Waking in my bed
I rushed downstairs,
And woke my mum and dad.
I went into the lounge,
And opened all my presents.
It felt so pleasant!

I am going to have a party.
All my friends and family will come.
I'll even give a cake to some.

Bouncing on my trampoline with everybody there
Even my little cousin with his toy Noddy
All the food is making me hungry
Let's get eating it in a hurry.
Everyone is enjoying the food
Which makes me in a good mood!

Blowing out the candles on my birthday cake
All the attention makes me shake.
I make a wish,
For a shiny new goldfish.
I think I'll call him happy
Because looks very snappy.

As all the people drive away
I go to my bed and that's where I'll stay.

The 31st of March is my special day
The 31st of March is my birthday.

Carla Tyrrell (9)
Cathedral Primary School, Motherwell

When I Am Tall

When I am tall and you are small,
There are so many things I can be,
So sit down comfy and listen to me.
My hopes and dreams shine down like beams
And stay in my head,
Even in bed!

I'll be a footballer you will see!
I'll be rich that's how I'll be.
Play for Man United score a goal,
Goal, goal, hat-trick hero,
The final score is 3-zero.

I'd like to act, be an actor.
Star in films, stage and screen
My fans will love me they'll be so keen,
They'll give an Oscar just for me.

I'd own Porsche and Lamborghini,
Designing cars really freely.

Then I'd be an athletic champion.
Relay races, hurdles and sprinting.
Up in the sky the sun is glinting.

But I'm not tall,
I'm really small.

Owen Leach (8)
Cathedral Primary School, Motherwell

When I Am Tall

When I am tall,
And trees are so small.
There are so many things
I can tell you.
My thoughts,
I wish could come true.
So pull up a chair,
With a little bit of flair.

An Olympic runner I shall be,
Just you wait and see.
I could be a popstar,
Whose chauffeur drives a fancy car.
What about a R 'n' B dancer with all the moves,
I think I've got quite the groove.
I want to be an actor,
Then I will star in the 'X-Factor'.
I will be an architect,
And leave all houses to perfect.
I want to be a hairdresser,
Not a hair messer!
I want to own my own salon
And be a Disney character called Mulan.

I will live in a mansion
And still have a passion for fashion.
Swimming pools, jacuzzi all the rest.
Only up my standard.
Best!

That's what I want to be
When I am 23!

Georgia Deerin (8)
Cathedral Primary School, Motherwell

The Great Excitement

Excitement looks like an explosion of fireworks right down from
my heart.
Excitement sounds like a sizzling, whistling, rocket taking off
Into the shining sky above the stars.
Excitement feels like the most beautiful thing in the whole wide world.
It tastes like crackling, sparkles sizzling in my mouth
And smells like a garden of roses sitting in a row.

Courteney Williamson (9)
East Plean Primary School, Stirling

The Loneliness Poem

Loneliness looks like a creepy dark tunnel.
Loneliness sounds like guns shooting, bombs exploding
And shotguns firing.
Loneliness feels like you are all alone in a haunted house.
Loneliness tastes like dark chocolate that's been in the fridge
for weeks.
Loneliness smells like a rotten fruit that's in a garbage bin.
Loneliness reminds me of a dog called Troy.

Darren Gerrard (9)
East Plean Primary School, Stirling

The Amazing Happiness

Happiness looks like a nice bright sun.
It sounds like when you crunch into an apple.
It feels like your heart pumping really fast.
It tastes like fresh cold orange juice.
It smells like sweet vanilla ice cream.
It reminds me of camping in Scotland.

Llyam Valentine (9)
East Plean Primary School, Stirling

Frightened

Frightened feels like you are in a huge dark tunnel all by yourself
With nobody around and no way out.
Frightened sounds like bats fluttering their wings up and down,
Up and down.
Frightened looks like a shadow following you up the hall.
Frightened tastes like horrible cockroaches.
Frightened smells like a raging hot fire.
Frightened reminds me of my first day of school.

Ryan Curran (9)
East Plean Primary School, Stirling

Happiness

Happiness looks like the bluest ocean in the world
It sounds like a football erupting with noise.
It feels like it is your first game for a football team.
It tastes like the strongest mint in the world.
It smells like my dad's aftershave.
It reminds me of my first goal.

Ivor Swan (9)
East Plean Primary School, Stirling

The Day I Felt Lonely!

Loneliness looks like you're in a dark tunnel
And nobody is with you.

Loneliness sounds like your friends having so much fun,
You can hear them but you can't see them.

Loneliness feels like you're in the town
And there's loads of people
And you don't know where to go.

Loneliness tastes like dark chocolate
That's been in a hot boiling pot for years.

Loneliness smells like slimy macaroni.

Zaynab Akhtar (9)
East Plean Primary School, Stirling

Lonely, The Feeling

Loneliness looks like you have got left out
And you're sitting by the green bins.

Loneliness, sounds like people saying, 'Go away,
You can't play.'

Loneliness, like you have not drank and you're swallowing
Your saliva.

Loneliness smells like crisps that have been lying in the bin
For two weeks.

Loneliness feels like you want to go and say, 'I'm playing.'

Loneliness reminds me of when I had no friends to play with.

Chelsea Hart Donald (9)
East Plean Primary School, Stirling

The Best Happiness

Happiness looks like brilliant creamy, creamy chocolate.
It sounds like the start of the best day.
It feels like a lovely posies' petals.
It tastes like a brilliant creamy cake.
It smells like a lovely flower.
It reminds me of the first day of school.

Megan Elvin (9)
East Plean Primary School, Stirling

Love

Love is red like a rose
It smells like chocolate
It feels like happiness
It reminds me of my father
It looks like roses
It tastes like candy canes
It sounds like birds singing.

Amy-Leigh McDade (10)
Greenhills Primary School, East Kilbride

Fear

Fear is purple like a terrible day
It smells like my grandad's house before he died
It looks like a picture of him feeling sick
It feels like a very hard rock
It sounds like a giant walking through the town
It reminds me of the sea swishing
It tastes like raw potatoes.

Samantha McLean (10)
Greenhills Primary School, East Kilbride

Anger

Anger is red like fire
It looks like my dad shouting
It reminds me of bad memories
It smells like smoke
It feels like slime
It tastes like bad carrots
It sounds like a drum banging.

Shannon Gair (11)
Greenhills Primary School, East Kilbride

Happiness

Happiness is yellow like the sun
It smells like fresh lemons
It feels like I'm with someone I love
It tastes like doughnuts
It sounds like birds tweeting
It looks like a little diamond
It reminds me of happy days.

Lauren McWhinnie (10)
Greenhills Primary School, East Kilbride

Happiness

Happiness is yellow like the sun shining in the sky
It looks like lovely love hearts
It feels like a soft silky pillow
It smells like a red rose
It tastes like a delicious chocolate bar
It reminds me of my mum giving me a hug
It sounds like the birds singing in the sun.

Kalina Ritchie (11)
Greenhills Primary School, East Kilbride

Happiness

Happiness is blue like the sky
It looks like the best present ever
It tastes like a hot pizza
It sounds like the waves crashing
It smells like chocolate
It feels like soap
It reminds me of all the good things from my past.

Ewan Gardiner (10)
Greenhills Primary School, East Kilbride

Fear

Fear is blue like ice
It smells like burning fire
It tastes like green olives
It reminds me of my dad shouting
It sounds like the wind blowing noisily
It looks like the stone-cold ice
It feels like crisp snow.

Amy Platt (11)
Greenhills Primary School, East Kilbride

Anger

Anger is orange like fire
It feels like flames burning
It sounds like flickering sparks
It reminds me of a burning hot fire
It tastes like smoke and burning
It looks like flames flying everywhere.

Sarah Sanders (10)
Greenhills Primary School, East Kilbride

Anger

Anger is scary like wolves
It reminds me of boxers
It feels like thunder crashing
It smells like burning coal
It sounds like someone screaming
It looks like an angry dog
It tastes like fire.

Josh Cecchetti (10)
Greenhills Primary School, East Kilbride

Love

Love is red like my heart
It feels like first love
It smells like my first chocolate bar
It tastes like my first drink when I'm thirsty
It reminds me of my first kiss
It sounds like my first laugh
It looks like people so happy.

Alicia McNab (11)
Greenhills Primary School, East Kilbride

A Boy

There was a boy who had a hat
He also had a pet rat
And no one knows why
The rat was so shy
And the rat got chased by the cat.

Stuart Frame (8)
Lenzie Primary School, Glasgow

A Boy Called Ben

There once was a fellow named Ben
He had a pet that was a hen
And he was the age of ten
Later he saw Sam
Who was very calm
And then he had a dancing pen.

Olivia Gibson (9)
Lenzie Primary School, Glasgow

The Sound Collector
(Inspired by 'The Sound Collector' by Roger McGough)

Afternoon comes with school bell ringing
Afternoon comes with cars vrooming
Afternoon comes with people laughing
Afternoon comes with children humming
Afternoon comes with teachers shouting
Afternoon comes with children screaming
Afternoon comes with the sun burning
Afternoon comes with dogs barking
Afternoon comes with girls farting.

Matthew Wan (8)
Lenzie Primary School, Glasgow

The Fellow Named Sam

There once was a fellow named Sam
Who was never taught to like ham
He once had a piece
And fell on his niece
Who went crazy and ate a lamb.

Ayan Shaukat (9)
Lenzie Primary School, Glasgow

Afternoon

Afternoon comes with lunch bells ringing
Afternoon comes with pencils writing
Afternoon comes with doors smashing
Afternoon comes with rainbows lightening
Afternoon comes with the sun whispering
Afternoon comes with babies chatting.

Inayah Jamil (9)
Lenzie Primary School, Glasgow

The Madman

I knew a man with smelly toes
He liked to pick his spotty nose
He fell in a pond
And found a fluffy wand
Then he went and broke a metal hose.

Saoirse Murdoch (8)
Lenzie Primary School, Glasgow

The Sound Collector
(Inspired by 'The Sound Collector' by Roger McGough)

Afternoon comes with lunch bell ringing
Afternoon comes with teachers shouting
Afternoon comes with cars zooming
Afternoon comes with children screaming
Afternoon comes with dogs barking
Afternoon comes with food splatting
Afternoon comes with sun burning
Afternoon comes with rain spitting
Afternoon comes with wind batting
Afternoon comes with water splashing
Afternoon comes with lights flashing
Afternoon comes with birds tweeting.

Gavin Williams (9)
Lenzie Primary School, Glasgow

The Clumsy Fellow

There once was a clumsy fellow,
He could never play the cello,
He had a friend Kay,
Who threw it away,
And bought a drum that was yellow.

Alex Tomkins (9)
Lenzie Primary School, Glasgow

Afternoon

Afternoon comes
With lunch bells ringing.

Afternoon comes
With brothers banging.

Afternoon comes
With school kids singing.

Afternoon comes
With school bells ringing.

Afternoon comes
With people pinging.

Afternoon comes
With kids growing.

Afternoon comes
With trains hooting.

Afternoon comes
With cars peeping.

Afternoon comes
With bees buzzing.

Findlay Clark (8)
Lenzie Primary School, Glasgow

The Wee Red Man

There once was a wee red man
Who fell in the frying pan
He lost his shoe
And didn't know what to do
Then had a fight with his gran.

Ben McLean (8)
Lenzie Primary School, Glasgow

Joyful

It is like a little bell in my heart,
A choir of angels and fairies
Fluttering around in the air.
It tastes like a baked cupcake
With fluffy icing and sprinkles.
It smells like candyfloss
And popcorn
The sweetest smell ever!
It feels like bubbles bubbling out
Of a Cola drink.
It reminds me of long, sweet,
Candy rock sparkling days.

Kim Ritchie (11)
Lumphinnans Primary School, Lumphinnans

Anger

Anger feels like being inside
A bottle of fizzy juice,
Being shaken and thrown and then
Opened.
It sounds like standing at the
Bottom of an erupting volcano,
Hearing all the people scream in
Terror and pain.
The taste of a sour, bitter lemon
Forming in your mouth,
A battlefield with thousands of
People going to war!
Anger!

Amy Moir (11)
Lumphinnans Primary School, Lumphinnans

Amazed

Amazed is like balloons popping around my head.
It sounds like a noisy room that just went quiet.
It tastes like jelly wobbling in my mouth.
It smells like chocolate aroma over my senses.
It feels like a person suddenly falling to the ground.
It reminds me of a choir dropping their mouth on a high note.
It is like not breathing when you're shocked and frightened.

Laura Brown (11)
Lumphinnans Primary School, Lumphinnans

Delighted

Today I woke up
Feeling delighted
Heard little children
Playing outside.

In my mouth
I tasted melting candyfloss
I smelt sweet roses outside.

I felt I had won
Millions of pounds
It reminded me of
When I was little.

But the best thing
About feeling like this
Is when I picture it
I see all my family together.

Caitlin Burns (11)
Lumphinnans Primary School, Lumphinnans

Puzzled!

It's like a question you can't answer.
You have to think long and hard about it.
It reminds me of someone
Stranded on an island.
It sounds like something being
Played in the wrong key.
It's all mixed up!
It feels weird; it feels bumpy like
It's out of proportion.
It looks like a jigsaw piece that
Doesn't fit.

Shannon Watson (11)
Lumphinnans Primary School, Lumphinnans

Jealous

Jealous is like a crack that
Separates you and the whole world.
An explosive substance about to burst,
Out of a deadly, diseased hole.
It smells like a revolting, ghastly odour.
It sounds like an ear splitting echo,
Booming in my head.
It tastes like an infected toxic powder,
It feels like a venomous snake bite.
It reminds me of a dreadful,
Beastly punishment,
Jealousy is like a destructive
Noxious beast!

Nicole Brogan (11)
Lumphinnans Primary School, Lumphinnans

Shy

Shy is like hiding behind locked doors
Unable to get out.
It sounds like a roaring audience
That's never roared so loud,
The taste is like dry hot sand
That makes you shiver.
It smells like a room of people's body heat
It feels like weights on my shoulders
And eyes all around me.
It reminds me of a stage when
Someone's on it,
They all stare!
Shy is like a straight ruler but
Snapped in half!

Nicole Moffat (11)
Lumphinnans Primary School, Lumphinnans

My Peaceful World

Peaceful feels like a soft breeze brushing past my face.
It feels like I'm lying on candyfloss.
All I hear is the sea, the waves,
And Holly and Cassie barking in excitement.
It tastes like a freshly baked, still warm baguette,
All I can smell is expensively melted chocolate,
It reminds me of delicious colourful jelly beans
Rustling in their wrappers.
When you're in my peaceful world,
You open your eyes and you can see soft, spongy, cushiony
Lily pads drifting down a river.
Now you have seen my peaceful world.
Now start thinking of yours.

Sarah Venters (12)
Lumphinnans Primary School, Lumphinnans

Peaceful

Peaceful is like falling into a nice
Fluffy cloud,
It sounds like a lot of birds singing,
Peaceful tastes like delicious,
Yummy chocolate.
It feels like a nice gentle wind
Across your face.
Peaceful reminds you of waking on
A nice sunny morning.
It's like lying down and looking at
The starlit night sky.
Peaceful!

Kelly Maxwell (11)
Lumphinnans Primary School, Lumphinnans

Hungry

So hungry I could eat a big fat horse,
My stomach rumbling like a volcano.
I dream of a big, fat juicy king rib,
My mouth is as dry as the sand in the desert,
Or a car stopping because it has run out of fuel.

Nathan Kernaghan (11)
Lumphinnans Primary School, Lumphinnans

Anger

It feels like a heavy weight,
Falling and crushing the life out of you.
It sounds like smashing glass
And it looks like fire.
The smell of smoke and taste of red-hot chilli.
It reminds me of a plane
Crashing in a film.
Anger.

Michael Sutherland (9)
Lumphinnans Primary School, Lumphinnans

Angry

Angry is just like a volcano about to erupt,
And I am in the middle.
I am going to explode!
I must get out of here!

It tastes like the worst food in the world!
Everything is mixed with fire!

Dylan Evans (10)
Lumphinnans Primary School, Lumphinnans

Peaceful

Peaceful sounds like birds singing softly,
It feels like I'm soaring into the sky.
Peaceful looks like someone asleep,
It smells like beautiful flowers.
Peaceful tastes like strawberries and chocolate dip,
It reminds me of daydreaming dogs
Twitching while they sleep.
Peaceful.

Brandon Henderson (10)
Lumphinnans Primary School, Lumphinnans

Peaceful

It sounds like the birds tweeting in the trees,
It feels like a big fluffy pillow,
It looks like flowers blooming in the hot summer sun.
Peaceful smells like a fresh baked cake,
And tastes of strawberries dipped in ice cream.
It reminds me of fish swimming in a pond,
Going round and round.

Rebecca McAllister (9)
Lumphinnans Primary School, Lumphinnans

Peaceful

It sounds like calm waves rolling through the sea,
It feels like smooth cotton candyfloss
Melting in my mouth.
It looks like melted chocolate running from a spoon,
It smells like beautiful roses in the garden.
Peaceful tastes like strawberries dipped in
Melted chocolate.
It reminds me of the water at the beach on holiday.

Chelsea Muir (9)
Lumphinnans Primary School, Lumphinnans

Peaceful

It sounds like the sea gently touching the rocks.
It makes me feel calm and cool like I'm in a trance.
It tastes like strawberries dipped in cream,
It smells like cakes made with lots of love.
It reminds me of my family,
And all the love they give me.
Peaceful.

Mhari Wilson (9)
Lumphinnans Primary School, Lumphinnans

Peaceful

It sounds like gentle waves rolling onto the beach,
It feels like soft fluffy candyfloss
Touching me gently,
It looks like melting chocolate in the oven,
It smells like lovely flowers in the garden.
Peaceful tastes like pancakes and ice cream,
It reminds me of going on holiday with my family,
And all the love they give to me.

Ailidh Ferguson (9)
Lumphinnans Primary School, Lumphinnans

Anger

Anger is the sound of clashing bricks,
It feels like a volcano erupting inside me.
It looks like a storming herd of bulls,
It smells of hatred and disgust.
It tastes like a burning fire inside my mouth.
It reminds me of a blazing fire,
That consumes the trees.
Anger.

Amy Simpson (9)
Lumphinnans Primary School, Lumphinnans

Peaceful

It sounds like a bird humming in the tree,
It smells like beautiful roses,
Just been picked.
It feels like melting ice cream in your mouth.
It tastes like soft, fluffy candyfloss,
It looks like a quiet country street,
It reminds me of lying on a beach on holiday.
Peaceful.

Amy Howie (9)
Lumphinnans Primary School, Lumphinnans

Anger

It feels like you're being ripped in half,
Anger sounds like symbols being clashed together.
It looks like a bright red warning light
Flashing in my head.
It smells of burning wood,
Anger tastes like you're swallowing a
Burning sword,
It reminds me of an exploding car in a film!
Anger!

Ryan Menzies (10)
Lumphinnans Primary School, Lumphinnans

Anger

It feels like a house falling down
On top of you!
It rips you apart,
Smashed and tearing you to pieces,
Like you were hit by thunder,
And your heart is on fire
It explodes and opens you up.
Eyes following you and you running away.

Rhys Connor (9)
Lumphinnans Primary School, Lumphinnans

Anger

Anger sounds like your heart exploding with rage.
It is the worst feeling ever.
Anger looks like a time bomb ready to go off.
It smells like burning ashes.
Anger tastes like black coal,
It reminds me of a black hole in space.

Christopher Davies (10)
Lumphinnans Primary School, Lumphinnans

Happy

It feels like you're gliding over the highest cloud
Or
Swimming in the deepest ocean.
It smells like fresh chicken nuggets,
It sounds like the waves hitting against the rocks.
It looks like a sunny day,
It tastes like candyfloss.

James Merrilees (9)
Lumphinnans Primary School, Lumphinnans

Happy

Like a bird flying in the sky,
Softly and calm like the waves.
Like the sun shining down on me.
I feel like a puffy white cloud
Making wonderful shapes in the sky.

Blair Jones (10)
Lumphinnans Primary School, Lumphinnans

Happiness

It sounds like birds whistling in the summer sky.
It feels like a big sponge cake.
It looks like a heavenly angel,
Everywhere it smells like melting chocolate,
Freezing on top of ice cream.
It tastes like a fluffy chocolate bar
And reminds me of my family at Christmas.
Have you got it?
Happiness.

Alisha McAllister (9)
Lumphinnans Primary School, Lumphinnans

Peaceful

Peaceful is like floating in an empty sea,
Hearing the soft waves ripple.
It sounds like a gentle breeze blowing through the fields,
Smelling like freshly cut grass with flourishing flowers,
The taste of a sweetly baked cake enters my mouth.
Peaceful feels like drifting into a world of your own,
A never-ending dream.
When I'm feeling like this it reminds me of a calm, clear blue sky.
I see the clouds slowly floating by.
When I picture peaceful I can see a heavenly gateaux
Just waiting to be tasted.

Natalie Wilson (12)
Lumphinnans Primary School, Lumphinnans

Springtime In Morningside

See lovely daffodils dancing.
I see a man cutting his lawn.
I see two aeroplanes flying through the air,
And I feel excited and happy.

I hear an alarm beeping and children chattering happily.
I hear the birds singing gracefully
And the trees rustling from side to side.
And I feel lovely and warm by the sun.

I smell smoke from a barbecue.
I smell petrol from cars and lunch in the hall
And I smell honey
And I feel refreshing.

I touch the flowers which smell beautiful,
I touch the dew on the grass and I touch a fluffy dog and a cat
And I feel excellent.

Erika Black (9)
Morningside Primary School, Wishaw

Springtime In Morningside

I see red roses swaying in the breeze.
I see blue cars shining in the sparkly sun.
I see birds singing in the shady trees,
And I feel great that spring is here.

I hear a lawnmower chipping grass,
I hear trees sizzling in the sun,
I hear footsteps on the hard ground,
And I feel good to be back.

I smell flowers that you have never smelled before.
I smell beautiful school food,
And I feel great.

I touch the great stone walls.
I touch the new varnished benches.
I touch the sparkling new car,
And I feel good that I can touch.

Mark Bradshaw (8)
Morningside Primary School, Wishaw

Springtime In Morningside

I see birds flying in-between the long branches,
Planes flying through the air and cars driving up the streets,
And I feel happy because I have eyes to see with.

I hear a lawnmower whizzing up and down the grass,
Birds tweeting in the sky,
Children laughing and giggling
And I feel very relaxed about that.

I smell the breeze of May,
The daffodils blowing my nose up and people cooking next door,
And I feel happy that I have a nose to smell.

I touch the wet and soggy leaves from that morning
And I feel happy that I have hands to touch with.

Grant Wood (9)
Morningside Primary School, Wishaw

Springtime In Morningside

I see daffodils starting to grow,
Cats enjoying the sun,
Birds flying happily around,
And I feel the sun hitting me instantly.

I hear a lawnmower cutting the grass,
Birds singing cheerfully, songs in the trees,
Cats hunting in the sun,
And I feel happiness coming my way.

I smell food going in school,
Daffodils blowing in the wind,
The trees blowing,
And I feel the wind blowing gently.

I touch the dew on the grass,
The daffodils' petals
Kittens just been born,
And I feel the daffodils as I pick them.

Katherine Colvin (9)
Morningside Primary School, Wishaw

Springtime In Morningside

I see the lovely yellow sun in the blue sky
The beautiful smelling flowers
The trees swaying in the breeze
And I feel great that springtime is here.

I hear a man cutting his grass
Teachers teaching the pupils
Birds tweety in the sky
And I feel the wind blowing.

I smell the lunch in the hall
Lovely flowers in the hills
Freshly cut grass
And I feel like a tree in the breeze.

I touch the freshly cut grass in the field
The hard bark on the trees
The wet flowers in the morning
And I feel like a house on a hillside.

Robert Crawford (9)
Morningside Primary School, Wishaw

Springtime In Morningside

I see a man mowing the grass
I see daisies dancing in the sun
I see the sun in a clear blue sky
And I feel happy because the sun is out.

I hear birds singing in the trees
I hear bees buzzing about
I hear cars driving on the road
And I feel great because God gave me the sense to hear.

I smell flowers in the garden
I smell honey in the bees' hive
I smell sausages cooking on the barbecue
And I feel fabulous because God gave me the sense to smell.

I touch soft dry grass
I touch hard bark on the tree
I touch wet dew on the soft grass
And I feel lovely because spring is here again.

Alastair Macfarlane (9)
Morningside Primary School, Wishaw

Springtime In Morningside

I see the sun in the blue sky
I see a man cutting the grass
I see cars passing by on the road
And I feel so happy.

I hear birds singing all day in the sky
I hear cars going by on the road all day
I hear a lawnmower cutting the grass
And I feel good.

I smell the school dinners coming into school
I smell the air in the sky
I smell the flowers on the grass
And I feel excited.

I touch the trees on the branches
I touch the school walls and they feel rough
I touch a fluffy cat
And I feel fine.

Lauren Daly & Lucy Burns (11)
Morningside Primary School, Wishaw

Summer Poem

I see children playing in a theme park
I see people going to Largs
I hear the birds go *tweet, tweet, tweet,* then I have a sweet
I hear the postman putting the mail through the mail box
I feel a summery green apple and it's round and juicy
I picked up a slimy tadpole
I taste the lovely sweet lollipop
I taste the lovely dripping ice cream.

Sophie Macinnes (9)
Murray Primary School, East Kilbride

A Summer Poem

I can see children having fun in a brightly-coloured park
I can see the sunny day take over the dark.

I can feel the warm air touch my hands
I can feel the crunchy, hard sand.

I can taste the ice-cold water touch my lips
I can taste the nice apple juice while I'm taking sips.

I can smell the lovely scent of flowers
I can smell the nice Haribo sours.

I can hear lots of children having fun at the fair
I can hear the birds tweeting while they are in the air.

Euan Hamilton (9)
Murray Primary School, East Kilbride

Summer Poem

I can hear the children laughing as they run around and play,
The sun is steaming hot and it's a summer's day.

I can smell the burgers from a barbecue,
It's coming from my garden, I'll invite you.

I can taste my ice cream, it's nice and cold,
But you can't get one because they're all sold.

I can feel the sun sizzling on my back;
I want to jump into a huge ice sack.

I can see the flowers blooming nice and bright,
If you look really carefully then it's a beautiful sight.

I love to go to the beach, the sun's so hot my skin's beginning
                                                                                to screech.

To get an ice cream is such a treat,
When I get one I just have to eat.

Do not worry summer's not over,
But it would be lucky if you found a four-leaved clover.

Ross MacGregor (10)
Murray Primary School, East Kilbride

Summer Poem

Young children crying because of suncream in their eyes,
Lots of children walking around because of no school,
Birds tweeting to each other,
Children screaming because they're in an ice-cold pool,
I jump in the sea like a bird diving in to get a fish,
I feel suncream getting put on my skin
Like the wind going gently across my face,
I can taste the ice-cold water running down my mouth,
I can taste the melting ice cream running slowly down my mouth,
I can smell my dad's lovely honey getting poured into my dad's coffee
I can smell the lovely flowers swaying from side to side,

My favourite part of summer is when there is no school.

James Nugent (10)
Murray Primary School, East Kilbride

My Mum

My mum has eyes of blue
With curly hair she is lovely too
I think of her all the time
Her teeth are like shiny dimes
She looks after me when I am ill
I love all the things she has bought
I love my mum
I'll love her forever
My love for her is in the love river.

Laura Gillies (10)
Murray Primary School, East Kilbride

In The Jungle

In the jungle, where the lions roar,
In the jungle, where the eagles soar,
In the jungle, far away from home.

In the jungle, where the trees are tall,
In the jungle, where the creatures call,
In the jungle far away from home.

In the jungle, where the monkeys swing,
In the jungle, where the rabbits spring,
In the jungle, far away from home.

In the jungle, where the tortoise crawls,
In the jungle, where they all make some noise,
In the jungle, far away from home.

Lara Wark (10)
Murray Primary School, East Kilbride

Shopping

S hopping is my favourite thing
H olidays are best to bargain things
O pen up your eyes and see someone shopping just like me
P uppies, purses, pink galore
P arades of people shoving through the door
I roning board up for sale
N ice panties hanging on the rail
G ang of people here to shop all day, long until they drop!

Nikki Forsyth (10)
Murray Primary School, East Kilbride

Storm At Sea

I foam! I rage! I bring destruction!
Sailors brave or courageous,
They all fall into my rages!
I am merciless in all my might!
I have no halo or ray of light!
I murder! I destroy! I kill
Women, men, girls and boys!
I have no silver lining!
I have no better half!
Unforgiving waves crash down on boats and ships!
I overturn them so they do marvellous flips!
But I calm eventually, I seem like calm seas and skies,
But this is just a clever disguise,
Inside I have evil eyes!

Bethan Mackie (11)
Murray Primary School, East Kilbride

My Heart

My heart is like an icy lake
On whose cold centre he stands.
The prince my heart he shall take,
And also take my hand.

To melt my heart is his aim
To keep me safe from harm
No one loves me just the same
His love now makes me warm.

The prince came on his charger
To take me far away
With his love my heart grew larger
He'll marry me today.

Alison Lovatt (10)
Murray Primary School, East Kilbride

Laughter

Laughter is yellow and green like a buttercup in the meadow.
It smells like a lily so pretty and fine.
She tastes like happiness very hard to find.
Sounds like a kiss on the cheek from the one most loved.
Feels like a tingle in your heart so hard to explain.
It lives under your tongue so you may use it any day.

Rebecca McNally (11)
Murray Primary School, East Kilbride

Summer Poem

In the summer I can see burning smoke from the barbecues coming
in front of me.
Up in the sky I can see a big, bright ball shining on me.
As I play with my blue bouncy ball I can hear birds tweeting like it's
in my ear.
I can hear children splashing in the shiny, blue water.
I can touch the suncream like it is ice cream melting in my hand.
I can touch the sand on my feet, it is like sugar.
I can smell the flower's pollen like a basket of fruit.
I can smell the burgers burning like the shimmery sun is melting.
I can taste the salt when I am in the sea like a bowl of sour sugar.
I can taste the candyfloss melting in my mouth like a cuddly cloud.

Emma Devine (9)
Murray Primary School, East Kilbride

Summer

In the summer the ice cream tastes so good.
In the summer children like to sunbathe for a good suntan.
In the summer the blossom it smells very lovely.
When it is hot touching the nice cold water is relaxing.
You can hear the birds singing in the summer.
I feel happy because in the summer the caravan we have water
fights.

Jennifer Mackie (9)
Murray Primary School, East Kilbride

Summer Poem

I see children screaming, their skin is burning.
I see smoke from people's gardens because they are having
barbecues.

I can hear children asking for ice cream
I can hear people jumping into swimming pools.

I can touch the water in a swimming pool
I can touch the green grass in the ground.

I can smell burgers in a barbecue
I can smell the fresh grass in the ground.

I can taste burgers straight from the barbecue
I can taste the grass scent in my mouth.

Owen Garrity (9)
Murray Primary School, East Kilbride

Summer Poem

The schools are out and we can see the flowers grow everywhere.
You can see the bouncy rabbits bouncing about your garden.
I hear the sea crashing against the rocky shore.
You hear the birds singing in the morning when you wake up.
You touch the crunchy sand at the beach.
In the summer at the beach you touch the bright, blue cold sea.
In the summer I smell the brown burned burgers that are on the hot,
                                                    warm barbecue.
The children smell the warm food burning when they play with their
                                                                               friends.

Kirstin Hosie (9)
Murray Primary School, East Kilbride

Summer Poem

In the summer holiday we have fun once a day.
We hear the birds go tweet, tweet, tweet
Then I have a lovely sweet.
The sun is beating down on me like I'm in the desert.
I'm getting warmer each step I take on this lovely journey.
I love the taste of sweet ice cream
It looks like snow but it tastes of cream.
I can see the dark blue waves
It looks so cold but I'm so warm, I'm going to take a shot.

Melissa Green (10)
Murray Primary School, East Kilbride

Summer Poem

Boys and girls swimming in a light blue pool and loving it.
People are sunbathing at the beach getting hot.
I love smelling flowers, it smells like perfume and have lovely colours.
Barbecues cooking sausages, smelling lovely.
Music is relaxing when it is smooth.
People talking about going on holiday.
Touching sand it feels hot. Swings are smooth.
Ice cream cools me down and melts on my tongue.

John Murphy (9)
Murray Primary School, East Kilbride

My Summer Poem

Summer is now here,
I can hear children singing like a bell ringing,
I can hear a bright, blue beach ball being bounced by happy, cheerful
children.
I can feel the hot sand touch my feet like I'm on the shining sun.
I can feel the heat of the sun like someone heavy sitting on me.
I can see people dancing around like it's a happy dancing disco.
I can see people sunbathing on the golden sugary sand.
I can smell hotdogs in the distance with a man shouting,
'Hotdogs for £1'
I can smell the fresh air on the big beach like a cold gentle breeze.
I can taste the candyfloss melting in my mouth like ice cream melting
in the sun.
I can taste the salt when I'm in the sea like I'm eating a big bag of
salt.

Robyn Graham (9)
Murray Primary School, East Kilbride

Summer Poem

I can hear children having fun in their back garden.
I can hear children playing with a beach ball in their swimming pool.
I can see a blue, calm sea making waves like a flood.
I can see the bright yellow sun shining on everyone.
I can feel hot sand burning my feet like I am on the sun.
I can feel cool, cold grass covering my feet like I am in Iceland.
I can smell the scent of peppermint off gigantic, great, green trees.
I can smell strong, salty water coming from the sea.
I can taste cold icy chocolate melting in my dry, drippy mouth.
I can taste a juicy ice-pole cooling my tongue down as cold as snow.

The sun is yellow and hot,
I am having fun in the summer,
I don't think winter is much fun,
But it is good that summer is here!

Courtney Smith (9)
Murray Primary School, East Kilbride

Summer Poem

I can see the tropical warm sunset shining on the clear blue sea,
Like a rainbow falling over me.
I can see the bright clear sky with the sun shining right in my eye.
I can taste brown, sugary chocolate ice cream like a long-lasting
sweet dream.
I can hear the roaring blue sea crashing onto seaweedish rocks
Almost covering my finally dried green socks.
I can hear the summer breeze annoying the leaves, also trying to
taunt and tease.
I can touch dew covered grass, I found a penny the colour of brass.
I can touch the sandy bay, I spy a donkey chewing on hay.

>Now that you've read
>My summer poem
>Go 'n' have a bath
>Filled with foam.

Emily McNeill (9)
Murray Primary School, East Kilbride

Summertime

People are going on holiday because it's warm
Lots of people are having lots of ice cream
People are having fun at the beach
People are going to the Dollan Baths because it is warm
Lots of people are having big water fights.

Josh Renicks (9)
Murray Primary School, East Kilbride

Summer Poem

I can hear bees buzzing and wasps whizzing like lawnmowers.
I can hear the birds singing in their nests that are in the beautiful
trees.

I can taste the summer ice cream melting like an iceberg,
I can taste all the summer strawberries like all the summer fruit.

I can see all the people getting burnt with tans
Like burnt toast crumbling.
I can see all the flowers growing like babies turning into kids.

I can smell the sweets coming from the summer sweet shops.
I can smell all the beautiful flowers.
I can feel the sand touching my hands like grit on the floor.
I can touch the core of the ice cream like crispy crunch crips.

Ewan Gamble (9)
Murray Primary School, East Kilbride

Summer Poem

The hot air blowing past my ears like someone whistling.
The waves crashing like the fizz of Coke.
I smell the hotdogs on the beach, they're coming from
                                              the hotdog shop.
I smell the sweet breeze of summer.
I see lots of people cheering and making lots of noise.
I see the leaves growing on the trees because summer is coming.
I touch the summer bee and it feels furry and soft.
When I touch the summer bee I feel its spiky hair.
I taste the chocolate ice cream, it tastes like ice.
I taste the ready salted crisps, they are very warm because of the
                                              sun and summer.

Conor Campbell (10)
Murray Primary School, East Kilbride

Summer Poem

I love hearing people having fun as they run around playing in the
    sun.
I can hear people having fun at parties.
I can see children having a water fight and they get a fright during
    the bright daylight.
I can see a barbecue cooking tasty burgers.
I touch the water of a swimming pool, it's glistening, shiny and blue.
I could touch the sun if I was a bird.

I smell my birthday cake on the 4th of July
Everyone enjoys it and so do I.
I can smell the shiny yellow suncream.
I can taste the ice in my mouth.
I can taste raspberry ripple in my mouth.
The sun is yellow, the sun is bright, and did you know,
Its name was Daylight.

Rebecca Bogle (9)
Murray Primary School, East Kilbride

Summer Poem

I can hear the bees buzzing like a lawnmower getting started.
I can hear burgers sizzling on an old rusty barbecue.

I can see the planes up in the sky going from place to place like
                                                an explorer.
I can see the ice cream drip, drip, dripping.

I can feel the greasy suncream on my arms and legs
I can feel the chocolate melting in my hand.

I can smell the chocolate ice cream in the crispy cone,
I can smell a burning barbecue.

I can taste the ice cream melting in my mouth
I can taste the hot summer air like I am eating a warm dinner.

Ellis Donald (9)
Murray Primary School, East Kilbride

My Aunty Angie

My aunty Angie is the funniest aunty in the world,
She likes to sing to Madonna while she does a twirl.

Saturday night is chocolate night,
She will give you a fright if you try to take a bite.

She is a cleanaholic, just loves to clean
Any time you mess stuff up, she starts to scream.

She loves cooking and shops in all the latest places,
She invites me over for dinner to play and stay.

She sits me down and talks to me,
And for all I love her, she loves me.

Kloi Graikos (10)
St Gregory's Primary School, Glasgow

My Granda Jimmy

My granda Jimmy is really unusual
Instead of a free Ford Focus he'd buy a Peugeot
At the talent show he had a bad cough
He forgot all the words to his song and got booed off.

He's not scared to show who he is
He really loves me and all his other grandkids
He said next year he's taking me to Spain
Even though he can be a pain.

He's a bit old to be a rock and roll star
But he doesn't care so he bought an electric guitar
He's a really good dancer
But he tries all difficult moves, I'd say he's a chancer.

Sean Hope (10)
St Gregory's Primary School, Glasgow

Spooky Castle

There's a spooky old castle inside my head . . .
With bats flying
Zombies spying
The floorboards creaking
Vampires peeking
Krights' armour walking
And skeletons talking.

Nicole Hampson (10)
St Gregory's Primary School, Glasgow

At The Seaside

Here I am sitting in the sun
Watching the children having fun
Swimming in the cool blue water
A lady bathing with her daughter
I shall go and join in, and have
A long and enjoyable swim.

Caitlin Mitchell (10)
St Gregory's Primary School, Glasgow

Unusual Mum

My mum thinks she's a popstar
She sings songs
Everywhere she goes.

Sometimes she even makes up
Her own songs,
And you can hear her at the other
Side of the world.

On Tuesday my mum goes to her gym
And she comes home
Very sparkly and thin.

At the end of the day
She's loving and caring
And helps me when I cry.

Stephanie Galloway (10)
St Gregory's Primary School, Glasgow

Spring!

S ugar plum fairies
P eople picking berries
R ed roses are growing
I nside or outside no breeze blowing
N ice flowers dancing in the sun
G irls and boys starting to run.

Shannyn Strickland (10)
St Gregory's Primary School, Glasgow

France

European country
Has national team
Makes grapes and wine
I've been there on holiday.

Fraser Yule (10)
Strathburn School, Inverurie

Kindness

Kindness, kindness
It looks like love
It feels like acceptance
It tastes like fresh grub
It smells like fresh baked bread
It sounds like love
Kindness is great.

Callum Jones (9)
Strathburn School, Inverurie

Cookies

A snack
Something I like
I want one now
I'm hungry; must eat now.

Alana Williams (9)
Strathburn School, Inverurie

Russell

My dad
Takes me out
Fun when we're together
I'll love my dad forever!

Hayley McKay (9)
Strathburn School, Inverurie

Chip

Chip
Is retired
She walks slowly
Loves to see me
She lives in Kelly's house.

Hannah Garden (10)
Strathburn School, Inverurie

Gomez

The cat
Is jet-black
He got run over
He went up to Heaven.

Jacqueline McKeown (9)
Strathburn School, Inverurie

Anger

Anger anger
It feels like being annoyed
It looks like a ghost
It smells like a car crash
It tastes like rotten food
It sounds like screaming girls
Anger is bad.

Greg Center (10)
Strathburn School, Inverurie

Anger, Anger

It feels bad
It looks like you are in a rage
It smells like paper burnt to a crisp
It tastes smoky
It sounds blazing and loud
Anger is *horrid!*

Nadia Inglis (10)
Strathburn School, Inverurie

Daydreams

Mrs Knox thinks I'm writing,
But I'm ballet dancing,
I'm up on my toes,
Dancing as elegantly as a swan,
And diving in the deep end of a pool,
Like a flying fish in the sea,
Now I'm watching my best friend is riding
Her favourite horse called Patch.

Mrs Knox thinks I'm reading
But I'm flying like an eagle in the sky,
And bouncing on a giant trampoline,
Now I'm riding a dolphin,
As it takes me to a secret island,
I'm eating a big banquet,
With so much food that it could fill a house,
Now I'm soaring in a plane,
Cutting through the air.

I'm partying with my friends,
In a giant limousine,
We stop off at a huge funfair,
I go on some rides,
But then I hear a very loud ringing,
I wake up,
Language is finished.

Rebecca Brown (11)
West Kilbride Primary School, West Kilbride

Autumn Days

I see spindly trees, slowly but surely becoming bare,
Their leaves limply twirling on their long journey down to the damp,
soggy ground.
The trees look like they are crying but still manage to look elegant
Surrounded by their crumpling leaves, like children departed.

I hear the wind whistling through the air like an invisible puppeteer,
Making the leaves swirl round in groups, rustling and crumpling into
Dust, crunching as they go.
The wind brings its howling sound like a wolf crying to the shining
Moon in a night as still and silent as one of the dark craters of the
Moon itself, everywhere it goes, like a loyal dog who loves to play.

I feel the sharp surface of the conker shell which is carried out of my
Reach by the non-stop wind which pierces my skin in one swift
Movement, like a dagger in the hands of a contract killer.
The bark on the naked trees is rough and wrinkled like old, dry skin
Hardened like a bone weak and dry with age.

I taste the sun-sweet berries growing on the rustling bushes.
Some are bright red and appealing, glinting in the sunlight,
But I leave them for the twittering birds singing a merry tune at
sunrise.
Some are purply-black and melt in your mouth, leaving you with a
Tingly feeling on your tongue, telling you to eat more of these
Luscious, mouth-watering berries.

I smell someone burning the ever falling leaves in their garden.
The smell shows the end of an era and the beginning of a new,
Like life and death.
As the smoke rises into the air, twirling and swirling up, up, up,
Until eventually fading away into the fresh, clean air.
The smell spreads far and wide, the wind bringing it as it goes,
Filling the world with a sense of loss with its dry, smoky smell,
Like a bonfire made of treasured possessions.

Rachael Miller (11)
West Kilbride Primary School, West Kilbride

Daydreams

Mrs Knox thinks I'm doing my work
But she's wrong.
I'm wrestling with crocodiles -
Three times my size.
I'm scuba diving in the Pacific Ocean - with great white sharks.
I'm swinging through the jungles of Indonesia with orangutans.

Mrs Knox thinks I'm paying attention
But again she's wrong
I'm ascending the climb -
Like Samuel Sanchez
I'm soaring through the air
Like a hen harrier
I'm flying through space in my spaceship
About to land on Saturn.

Mrs Knox thinks I'm researching
But I'm not
I'm sitting on my throne -
Just like Spartacus
In fact I am Spartacus
All my servants must obey unless they will be executed,
'Mussels for dinner please' I shout
I wake up
Suddenly I'm only sitting on a school chair not a throne.

Gordon Wilson (11)
West Kilbride Primary School, West Kilbride

Senses Of Autumn

I see . . .
The colours of autumn like scarlet, chestnut brown
And more yellow than a banana.
I see the helicopters twirling down from the almost bare tree.

I feel . . .
The crunchy leaves floating down skimming my face
And the strong wind rushing against my face like waves
Pushing against the sandy beaches.

I hear . . .
The wind quietly whistling and squirrels scurrying along the soft
Ground and crunchy dry leaves being crumbled by small children.

I smell . . .
Men burning their dry leaves and resin breaking out of the trees' bark.

I taste . . .
The delicious autumn apples and the lovely chestnut brown
                                                                                    chestnuts.

Clark Ferguson (11)
West Kilbride Primary School, West Kilbride

Autumn Days

I see . . .
The leaves twirling down from the tree, all different colours,
Amber, scarlet and chestnut brown.
I see . . .
Helicopters flying swiftly about the autumn sky and then landing
on the floor.
I see . . .
Conkers lying amongst leaves on the floor spiky and smooth ones.

I feel . . .
The wind blowing leaves against my face very gently.
I feel . . .
The leaves being scattered around my feet.
I feel . . .
My face getting nippy by the wind blowing my face.

I hear . . .
The wind whistling through my ears.
I hear . . .
Leaves crunching with people walking over them.
I hear . . .
Birds singing while flying through the sky.

I taste . . .
The apples from the trees.
I taste . . .
The brambles being picked for someone to eat.
I taste . . .
The chestnuts cooking on a fire.

Melissa Coby (11)
West Kilbride Primary School, West Kilbride

Daydreams

Mrs Knox thinks I'm concentrating
But I'm fighting dragons
As big as mountains,
I'm swimming with sharks
With teeth as big and sharp as knives,
I'm swinging in the jungle
With the gorillas as hairy
As a furry jacket,
I'm trying to take over the world
With my robot, which is as clever as a scientist.

Mrs Knox thinks I'm listening
But I'm not
I'm sliding down a slide
In a waterpark,
I'm flying into space
And land on Pluto,
I am driving a racing car,
Which is as fast as lightning,
I am crossing a tightrope at the circus
Which is as scary as a really, scary movie.

I am flying with ducks
I am running through a cave
Which is as long as ten limousines
I hear my name being called
Kerr, Kerr, Kerr, I wake up and
I see a pair of eyes and it's the teacher's
Right in front of my nose.

Kerr Wilson (11)
West Kilbride Primary School, West Kilbride

What's In The Box?

Is it
A wiggly worm wiggling
A silly spider stealing
A lazy ladybird lying
A beautiful butterfly bowling
A slow slug skipping
An angry ant acting.

Kate Parker (8)
West Kilbride Primary School, West Kilbride

Presents

P erfect slippers
R ound chocolates
E xcellent footballs
S pooky books
E normous silly teeth
N ice teddies
T iny rocking horses
S hiny bikes.

Sam Edwards (7)
West Kilbride Primary School, West Kilbride

What's In The Box?

Is it
A wiggly worm whispering
A bad butterfly bowling
An angry aphid acting
A silly slug stealing
A stupid spider skipping
A famous fly failing.

Fraser Murray (7)
West Kilbride Primary School, West Kilbride

What's In The Box?

Is it
An amazing aphid acting
A bouncy bluebottle buzzing
A drunk daddy longlegs dying
A grumpy grasshopper growling
A fashionable fly flying
A stinky slater scaring.

Caitlin McMail (7)
West Kilbride Primary School, West Kilbride

Limerick

There once was a man called Jim,
Who liked mac 'n' cheese out a tin.
He was a good man
Who drove a big van
And always put things in the bin.

Thomas Orr (8)
West Kilbride Primary School, West Kilbride

Limerick

I went to the movies with Molly.
Me and her played with my dollies.
We met up with Robbie
Robbie had bobby
Then I met up with Polly.

There once was a man from France
Who had a pet called Prance
He went to the bin
And ate up his din
But didn't have any romance!

Erin English (8)
West Kilbride Primary School, West Kilbride

Limerick

I went to the circus one day
Even the monkeys have to pay
I like the clowns
But then there's the hounds
Who ate all the horse's hay.

Abbie Fairclough (8)
West Kilbride Primary School, West Kilbride

A Garden Is . . .

A greedy caterpillar munching leaves
A kind bee drinking nectar
A huge shady tree swaying in the wind
A lovely rabbit crunching carrots
An apple tree getting picked
A shallow pond shining in the sun
A stag beetle hunting in the grass
An evil spider spinning a silky web
A bunch of children playing on a trampoline.

Jacob McBain (8)
West Kilbride Primary School, West Kilbride

A Garden Is . . .

A scent of flowers
A bouncy trampoline
A swinging seat
A bumpy slide
A spider spinning webs
A little lily ladybird
A lovely, lovely rose.

Josef Bacon (7)
West Kilbride Primary School, West Kilbride

A Garden Is . . .

A spotty ladybird crawling on a green leaf
A colourful flower in a red pot
A wiggly caterpillar munching crunchy leaves
A swinging seat that goes very high
A furry squirrel climbing up a tree
Crunchy carrots all in a lovely row
A stripy bee making lots of lovely honey
A spider spinning a silky web
Children playing all day long.

Emily McAlpine (8)
West Kilbride Primary School, West Kilbride

A Garden Is . . .

A happy child swinging
A huge tree shading the ground
A berry bush waving in the sun
A beautiful butterfly flying
A bouncy rabbit bouncing happily
A busy bee working hard
A happy child swinging.

Ross Maclean (7)
West Kilbride Primary School, West Kilbride

A Garden Is . . .

A hopping rabbit having fun
A silver web shining in the light
A cheeping bird in the tree
A swing swinging back and forth
A fountain pouring water all over the place
A black spider in a silver web.

Cerys Seaton (8)
West Kilbride Primary School, West Kilbride

A Garden Is . . .

A wiggly worm playing in the grass
A sweet smelling red flower popping out in a garden
A shady apple tree blowing in the wind
A busy bee stinging people
A flipping frog flipping in the pond
A gooey snail sliding on the path
A spotty parasol blowing in the fresh air
A forget-me-not bench.

Emma Turner (7)
West Kilbride Primary School, West Kilbride

Japanese - Haikus

Autumn leaves
Golden by the touch
Always falling off the trees
By spring they are green.

Winter
Kids making snowmen
Snowflakes falling on the ground
Always wrap up warm.

Heather McClymont (11)
West Kilbride Primary School, West Kilbride

My Japanese Haikus

The Waves
The waves sway smoothly
And colourful fish go by
The waves start to dance.

The Wind
Gliding through the trees
The wind whistles calm and smooth
It runs through my hair.

Dead Leaves
The dead leaves fall down
Onto a bundle of twigs
They blow off alone.

Sarah Wanless (11)
West Kilbride Primary School, West Kilbride

Japanese Haikus

Rain
From the clouds it comes
It patters on the rooftops
Puddles everywhere.

Sun
Its beams burning down
We know that summer is here
Glowing red and gold.

Wind
Blowing past the trees
Gusts of wind turn into storms
Whistling in my ear.

Thunder
Rumbles in the clouds
It strikes fear into our hearts
Rumble, crash then boom.

Sarah Davies (11)
West Kilbride Primary School, West Kilbride

Japanese Haikus

The Owl
A gliding shadow
With unblinking yellow eyes
Swoops then dives, then kills.

Fire
Dancing flames of gold
The wood changes to ashes
A glow of colour.

Spring
Buds come bursting out
Colour everywhere we look
New life has begun.

Iceberg
Liquid to solid
It will kill you if it can
Heat melts its cold heart.

Animals
They are all unique
Some have fur and some have skin
But all beautiful.

The Sea
Rushing waves storm past
You can't describe the colour
Creatures live beneath.

Jonathan Revie (11)
West Kilbride Primary School, West Kilbride

At The Chip Shop

Behind me stood
A tall dark haired man
With bushy black eyebrows
Small pebble-brown eyes
White shiny teeth
Smiling at me
He said to me,
'Whit you up tae?'
I said, 'Nothing much.'

'I better be going now.'
And he walked out the door.

Amy Hands (10)
West Kilbride Primary School, West Kilbride

A Lassie Poem

This loyal collie
Will stay by your side
When you're lost
She'll be your guide
Whenever you need her
Wherever she roams
Just call out
Lassie, come home.

Catherine Bacon (10)
West Kilbride Primary School, West Kilbride

At The Airport

A tall man,
Standing next to me,
Was wearing black, shiny shoes
Long linen trousers,
That were trimmed with gold silk thread.
A black coat,
Trimmed with red,
And gold buttons,
Wearing a badge.
His eyes were blue,
Thin brown eyebrows,
Wearing a black hat.
He said, 'I'll be flying you today.'
'Really, I would never have guessed!'
I replied sarcastically.

Ross Wilson (10)
West Kilbride Primary School, West Kilbride

At The Pub
A tall skinny man
Wearing a small black hat
Black Oxford shoes
He also had black trousers on
With an old brown belt
A frilly jacket on
He says, 'Want a pint mate?'
I said, 'No' and laughed.

Tom Hunt (10)
West Kilbride Primary School, West Kilbride

Walking To School

W alking to school keeps you cool
A walk a day will keep the doctor away
L et your legs do the walking while you do the talking
K eeps your hearty heart healthy
I nteresting sights and sounds can be found
N othing compares to all that fresh air
G arage the car, the walk's not too far.

Rachel Stirling (11)
West Kilbride Primary School, West Kilbride

Down The Mines

I'm down in the mines hurrying along,
With a coal cart attached to my waist.
It's extremely dark and damp down here,
And I'm finding it hard to take a breath.
I can hear a rat scurrying past,
I'm so scared and I've got to go fast.
I can't see where I'm going,
It's all so dark,
I wonder if I'll ever see the end?

Jennifer Green (11)
West Kilbride Primary School, West Kilbride

Down In The Coal Mines

I'm down here, sitting in the dark
I can hear a drip, drip, drip,
And I can see the scurrying rats.
I don't like sitting here,
Shivering and lonely,
The hurriers keep tricking me
They say that there's a ghost.
It's dusty and dirty
And scary sitting here
Oh how I wish that
My parents were rich.

Gemma MacMaster (11)
West Kilbride Primary School, West Kilbride

The Trapper's Poem

I'm sitting in this tunnel,
Beside this door
I can just make out rats
That are scuttling along the floor.

Over in the corner,
I can see a spider's web.
Oh I really don't like spiders
Oh I wish that I was dead.

Right, here comes the hurrier,
I'd better open this door, quick!
He won't even say thank you,
This job makes me sick.

The atmosphere is gloomy
I am very lonely
How I wish that they would make
This mine a bit more homely.

I can hear a huge bat
Flapping overhead
I'm upset and I'm dirty
And I really need my bed.

I just want to shout out loud
When will this cruelty stop?
I feel a drip from the ceiling
It just went down my top
Why must I do this job?

Emily Brittan (11)
West Kilbride Primary School, West Kilbride

The Trapper

Rats and hurriers scurry past me
That is what I see
Tap, tap, scratch, loud and clear
That is what I hear
Gas and soot like the pits of Hell
That is what I smell
I'm exhausted and I need a drink
That is what I think
I want to be home, it's so gloomy in here
That is the atmosphere.

Euan Mitchell (11)
West Kilbride Primary School, West Kilbride

A Trapper

Blackness all around in the cold, mouldy mine.
A sound growing louder, as it comes closer I open the door.
A strong sweaty smell goes past and a cool fresh air rushes by.
I go off in a dream, in a soft, warm bed of my own.
I quickly wake up and close the door.
It's dull and tiring and you can hear people in pain.
I feel terror as I see an explosion in the tunnel.
I close the door and quickly crawl for my life.
I reach the bucket and get pulled up.
Thank goodness I'm alive.

Katie Powell (11)
West Kilbride Primary School, West Kilbride

An Autumn Day

I hear . . .
The flapping of a robin, the creak from a tree.
I can hear the rustle of the leaves I fling into the air,
The tap of a fast squirrel.

I feel . . .
The rough scrape of the bark on a tree standing tall.
I feel the soft delicate tail of a red squirrel
And the jagged spikes of an unbroken conker lying on
the millions of leaves.

I see . . .
The strange and queer rotating fall of the helicopter leaves.
I look and I see bare trees with the leaves all lying in a heap beneath it
And I see sap dripping with grace towards the wet and damp ground.

I smell . . .
Resin and pine leaves from every direction.
I look, I smell the fresh autumn air drifting past my body
in a nice pleasant manner.
I can also inhale the beautiful smell of a fire lit and blazing bright
in the lovely forest.

I taste . . .
The chestnuts sweet and full of autumn flavours all in one.
I taste resin fresh from a tree that towers above the ground
full of life the apples thump on the ground.
I taste it, it is the perfect autumn flavour.

Sean Rees (11)
West Kilbride Primary School, West Kilbride

Trapper In The Coal Mine

Nothing but darkness looms in the air,
So there's not anything I can see without gloominess,
Here comes the rumble of the wheels on the coal cart,
Now I know the hurrier is struggling on.
There's a stench in the air from the scurrying rats,
That squeak all day long.
Just thinking of an explosion gives me shivers all over,
I hope I survive today.
I feel exhausted; this work is so awful,
I could just fall asleep . . .

Iona Lennie (11)
West Kilbride Primary School, West Kilbride

Young Writers Information

We hope you have enjoyed reading this book - and that you will continue to enjoy it in the coming years.

If you like reading and writing poetry drop us a line, or give us a call, and we'll send you a free information pack.

Alternatively if you would like to order further copies of this book or any of our other titles, then please give us a call or log onto our website at www.youngwriters.co.uk

**Young Writers Information
Remus House
Coltsfoot Drive
Peterborough
PE2 9JX
(01733) 890066**